Daily *warm-ups*

ANALOGIES

J. WESTON
WALCH
PUBLISHER
Portland, Maine

Purchasers of this book are granted the right to reproduce all pages.
This permission is limited to a single teacher, for classroom use only.

Any questions regarding this policy or requests to purchase further
reproduction rights should be addressed to:

Permissions Editor
J. Weston Walch, Publisher
321 Valley Street • P.O. Box 658
Portland, Maine 04104-0658

1   2   3   4   5   6   7   8   9   10
ISBN 0-8251-4321-7

The Daily Warm-Ups series is a wonderful way to turn extra classroom minutes into valuable learning time. The 180 quick activities—one for each day of the school year—review, practice, and teach word analogies. These daily activities may be used at the very beginning of class to get students into learning mode, near the end of class to make good educational use of that transitional time, in the middle of class to shift gears between lessons—or whenever else you have minutes that now go unused. In addition to providing students with structure and focus, they are a natural path to other classroom activities involving vocabulary or critical thinking. As students build their vocabularies and become more adept at analogy problem-solving, they will be better prepared for the standardized tests, such as the PSAT and SAT, that include analogy problems.

Daily Warm-Ups are easy-to-use reproducibles—simply photocopy the day's activity and distribute it. Or make a transparency of the activity and project it on the board. You may want to use the activities for extra-credit points or as a check on the critical-thinking skills that are built and acquired over time.

However you choose to use them, *Daily Warm-Ups* are a convenient and useful supplement to your regular lesson plans. Make every minute of your class time count!

What Is an Analogy?

An **analogy** is a statement in which two word pairs share the same relationship.

For example: *Captain* is to *boat* as *pilot* is to *airplane*.

The *captain* is the person who controls a *boat*, just as a *pilot* is the person who controls an *airplane*. Each pair of words fits into the same simple sentence that directly explains the relationship between the words.

1

Analogy Tips

A typical analogy looks like this:

finger : hand :: toe : foot

The colon (:) means "is to" and the double colon (::) means "as." The analogy is read "*Finger* is to *hand* as *toe* is to *foot*."

Write three similar analogies below.

Types of Analogies

Here are 10 types of analogies and examples.

Type	Examples
1. object/person : description	fire : hot
2. agent : object	artist : brush
3. agent : action *or* object : function	doctor : heal,
	closet : store
4. object/description/action : greater/lesser size or degree	tap : bang, glad : ecstatic
5. person/object : location	judge : court
6. cause : effect	ignite : burn
7. part : whole	sailor : navy
8. object/person : category	elm : tree, thief : criminal
9. word : synonym	lukewarm : tepid
10. word : antonym	hot : cold

© 2002 J. Weston Walch, Publisher

Relationship Sentences

The best way to figure out the relationship between a pair of words is to create a **relationship sentence.** A relationship sentence is a simple sentence that clearly shows the relationship between the two words. Write a relationship sentence using the following word pair: elm : tree

Think: "An *elm* is a type of *tree*."

4

Test: Which of the following two word pairs is the correct analogy?

rose : flower   grass : meadow

Plug each word pair back into the relationship sentence:

Write: Relationship sentences: A *rose* is a type of *flower*. That makes sense. A *grass* is a type of *meadow*. That doesn't make any sense.

The correct answer is elm : tree :: rose : flower.

Sometimes a relationship sentence isn't specific enough the first time around. When that happens, the relationship sentence needs to be adjusted. Here's an example:

bird : nest :: _____ : _____

(a) goose : duck   (c) water : ripple
(b) tree : forest   (d) bear : cave

A relationship sentence for **bird : nest** might be, "A bird lives in a nest." Test each choice by plugging it into the relationship sentence.

(a) A goose lives in a duck? No way.
(b) A tree lives in a forest? Maybe—but keep checking.
(c) A water lives in a ripple? No.
(d) A bear lives in a cave? That sounds like it could be right, too.

Write a more specific relationship sentence. Make the relationship between the two words clear.

Choose the correct word to

complete the analogy.

---

tired : exhausted :: _____ : furious

(a) calm

(b) unhappy

(c) angry

(d) amused

What type of analogy is this?

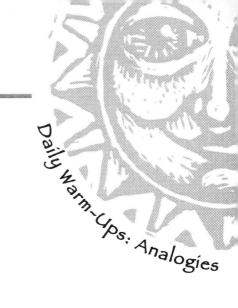

Choose the correct word to complete the analogy.

brake : _____ :: motor : run

(a) stop

(b) increase

(c) roll

(d) ride

What type of analogy is this?

.

Fill in the blank with a word that will complete the analogy. There are many correct answers.

mallard : duck :: _____ : tree

Write the relationship sentence you used to complete this analogy.

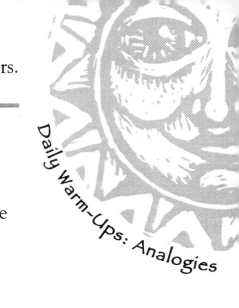

8

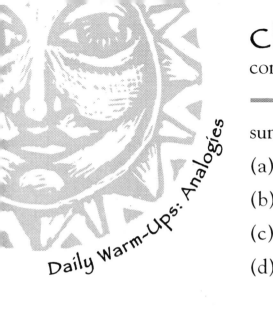

Choose the correct word pair to complete the analogy.

summon : dismiss :: _____ : _____

(a) call : reply

(b) intend : try

(c) intervene : meddle

(d) gather : disperse

What type of analogy is this?

Fill in the blanks with words that will complete the analogy. There are many correct answers.

chide : scold :: _____ : _____

Write the relationship sentence you used to complete this analogy.

10

Choose the correct word pair to complete the analogy.

pacify : calm :: _____ : _____

(a) identify : mysterious

(b) fortify : strong

(c) testify : suspicious

(d) mortify : happy

Write the relationship sentence you used to complete this analogy.

11

Choose the correct word to complete the analogy.

concur : disagree :: comprehend : _____

(a) forget

(b) learn

(c) misunderstand

(d) envision

Write the relationship sentence you used to complete this analogy.

Complete the analogy by choosing
the correct word from the word bank.

sculptor painter athlete gourmet dancer

chef : food :: _____ : clay

What type of analogy is this?

13

Choose the correct word pair to complete the analogy.

rural : bucolic :: _____ : _____

(a) urban : countrified

(b) endangered : safe

(c) evolved : regressed

(d) convoluted : twisted

14

Write the relationship sentence you used to complete this analogy.

Fill in the blanks with words that will complete the analogy. There are many correct answers.

liar : untruthful :: _____ : _____

Write the relationship sentence you used to complete this analogy.

Choose the correct word pair to complete the analogy.

skater : rink :: _____ : _____

(a) climber : gear

(b) explorer : adventure

(c) runner : track

(d) walker : shoe

16

Write the relationship sentence you used to complete this analogy.

Fill in the blank with a word that will complete the analogy. There are many correct answers.

nudge : shove :: glance : _____.

Write the relationship sentence you used to complete this analogy.

17

Choose the correct word pair to complete the analogy.

guardian : watch :: _____ : _____

(a) firefighter : ignite

(b) scribe : write

(c) scout : follow

(d) actor : imply

Write the relationship sentence you used to complete this analogy.

18

Choose the correct word to complete the analogy.

hungry : _____ :: annoyed : outraged

(a) satiated

(b) prepared

(c) uncomfortable

(d) ravenous

Write the relationship sentence you used to complete this analogy.

.

19

© 2002 J. Weston Walch, Publisher

Choose the correct word pair to complete the analogy.

engorge : fill :: _____ : _____

(a) assert : deny

(b) deploy : regain

(c) encourage : block

(d) initiate : begin

What type of analogy is this?

20

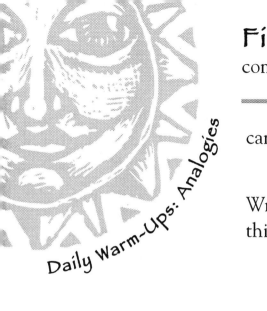

Fill in the blanks with words that will complete the analogy. There are many correct answers.

carelessness : mistakes :: _____ : _____

Write the relationship sentence you used to complete this analogy.

21

© 2002 J. Weston Walch, Publisher

Choose the correct word pair to complete the analogy.

sentences : paragraph :: _____ : _____

(a) notes : melody

(b) books : scholar

(c) questions : inquiry

(d) flowers : menagerie

22

Write the relationship sentence you used to complete this analogy.

Choose the correct word to complete the analogy.

_____ : vision :: sage : wisdom

(a) chief

(b) oracle

(c) rogue

(d) vagrant

Write the relationship sentence you used to complete this analogy.

23

© 2002 J. Weston Walch, Publisher

Fill in the blanks with words that will complete the analogy. There are many correct answers.

pig : sty :: _____ : _____

Write the relationship sentence you used to complete this analogy.

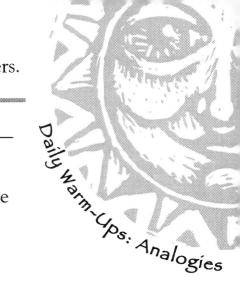

24

Choose the correct word pair to complete the analogy.

awl : tool :: _____ : _____

(a) garden : plant

(b) tributary : desert

(c) mast : warning

(d) automobile : vehicle

What type of analogy is this?

Fill in the blank with a word that will complete the analogy. There are many correct answers.

doctrine : credo :: _____ : glee

Write the relationship sentence you used to complete this analogy.

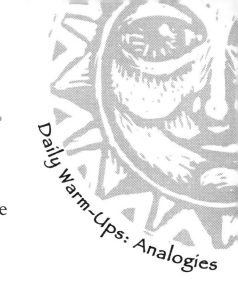

26

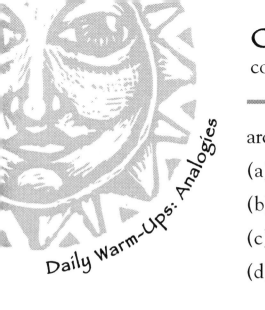

Choose the correct word pair to complete the analogy.

architect : blueprint :: _____ : _____

(a) gardener : fertilizer

(b) watchdog : leash

(c) navigator : map

(d) detective : culprit

What type of analogy is this?

Complete the analogy by choosing
the correct word from the word bank.

| wheel   vehicle   trail   tread   mountain |

fork : utensil :: bicycle : _____

Write the relationship sentence you used to complete
this analogy.

28

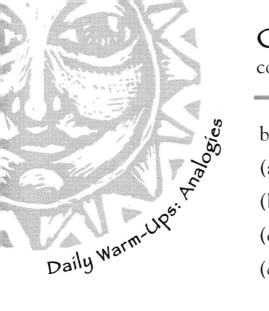

Choose the correct word pair to complete the analogy.

benefactor : donation :: _____ : _____

(a) imitator : comedy

(b) mediator : argument

(c) judge : ruling

(d) plaintiff : defense

Write the relationship sentence you used to complete this analogy.

29

Fill in the blanks to complete the analogy.

There are many correct answers.

---

trickle : gush :: _____ : _____

Write the relationship sentence you used to complete this analogy.

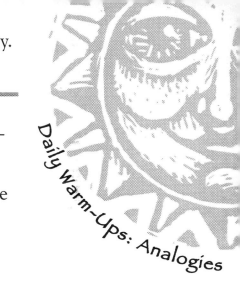

Choose the correct word to complete the analogy.

spark : ignite :: _____ : change

(a) catalyst

(b) experiment

(c) reaction

(d) exertion

Write the relationship sentence you used to complete this analogy.

.

31

Complete the analogy by choosing
the correct answer from the word bank.

halt	impair	converge	claim	entail

cease : _____ :: chase : pursue

Write the relationship sentence you used to complete this analogy.

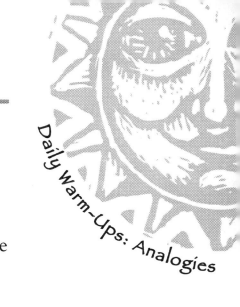

32

Complete the analogy. There will be more than one correct answer.

---

desert : arid :: rainforest : _____

Write the relationship sentence you used to complete this analogy.

© 2002 J. Weston Walch, Publisher

Choose the correct word pair to complete the analogy.

surplus : dearth :: _____ : _____

(a) transaction : coin

(b) reunion : family

(c) confusion : clarity

(d) quantity : quality

What type of analogy is this?

34

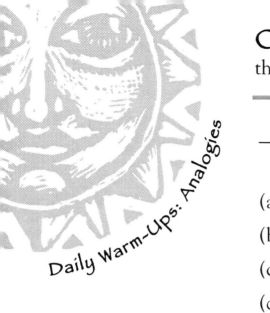

Complete the analogy by choosing the correct word.

_____ : rain :: drifts : snow

(a) sun

(b) puddles

(c) plows

(d) umbrellas

Write the relationship sentence you used to complete this analogy.

35

Fill in the blank to complete the analogy.

complainer : _____ :: climber : ascend

(a) gripe

(b) solve

(c) annoy

(d) assert

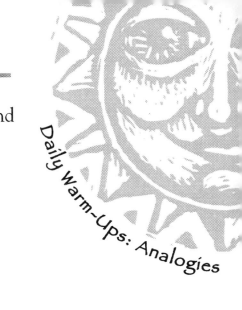

What type of analogy is this?

36

Complete the analogy by choosing
the correct answer from the word bank.

---

chord	podium	microphone	oration	lecture

dancer : stage :: speaker : _____

Write the relationship sentence you
used to complete this analogy.

© 2002 J. Weston Walch, Publisher

Fill in the blank to complete the analogy.
There is more than one correct answer.

---

actor : cast :: singer : _____

Write the relationship sentence you used to complete this analogy.

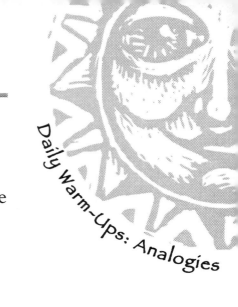

38

Choose the correct word pair to

complete the analogy.

---

surprise : shock :: _____ : _____

(a) stone : brick

(b) miser : spendthrift

(c) fear : terror

(d) happiness : sadness

Write the relationship sentence you
used to complete this analogy.

Fill in the blanks to complete the analogy.

There is more than one correct answer.

---

embellish : decorate :: _____ : _____

Write the relationship sentence you used to complete this analogy.

40

Choose the correct word to

complete the analogy.

---

sharpener : _____ :: megaphone : amplify

(a) glean

(b) emphasize

(c) point

(d) hone

Write the relationship sentence you used to complete this analogy.

41

Choose the correct word pair to complete the analogy.

biologist : laboratory :: _____ : _____

(a) painter : studio

(b) baker : oven

(c) engraver : metal

(d) forecaster : weather

What type of analogy is this?

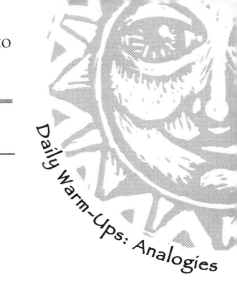

Choose the correct word to

complete the analogy.

trumpet : brass :: clarinet : _____

(a) violin

(b) orchestra

(c) woodwind

(d) music

Write the relationship sentence you used to complete this analogy.

.

43

© 2002 J. Weston Walch, Publisher

Fill in the blanks to complete the analogy.

There are many correct answers.

_____

_____ : _____ :: vendor : sell

Write the relationship sentence you used to complete this analogy.

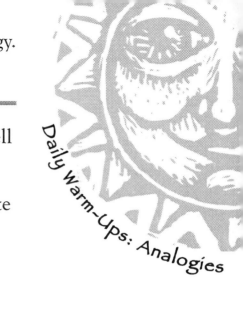

44

Choose the correct word to complete the analogy.

launch : lift :: thwart : _____

(a) incur

(b) fail

(c) douse

(d) remain

Write the relationship sentence you used to complete this analogy.

45

Complete the analogy by choosing
the best answer from the word bank.

---

utilize	impair	participate	unite	oversee

supervisor : _____ :: interpreter : translate

Write the relationship sentence you used to complete this analogy.

46

Fill in the blanks to complete the analogy.
There is more than one correct answer.

---

enigma : mysterious :: comedy : _____

What type of analogy is this?

47

Fill in the blanks to complete the analogy.

There are many correct answers.

---

sheer : opaque :: _____ : _____

Write the relationship sentence you used to complete this analogy.

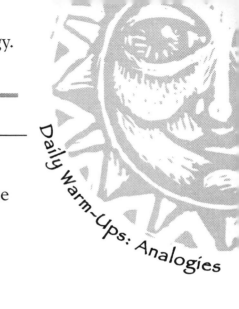

48

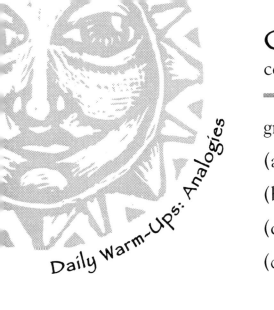

Choose the correct word pair to complete the analogy.

grain : silo :: _____ : _____

(a) glass : jar

(b) tire : automobile

(c) gasoline : tank

(d) air : atmosphere

Write the relationship sentence you used to complete this analogy.

49

Choose the correct word to complete the analogy.

botanist : plants :: _____ : rocks

(a) meteorologist

(b) geologist

(c) astronomer

(d) anthropologist

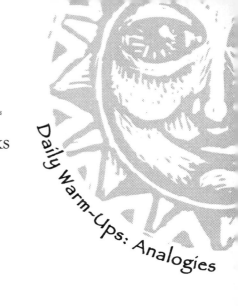

50

Write the relationship sentence you used to complete this analogy.

Complete the analogy by choosing
the correct answer from the word bank.

understanding   frustration   perfection
implication   determination

exploration : discovery :: inquiry : _____

Write the relationship sentence you used
to complete this analogy.

51

© 2002 J. Weston Walch, Publisher

Complete the analogy by filling in
the blanks. There are many correct answers.

_____ : _____ :: player : team

What type of analogy is this?

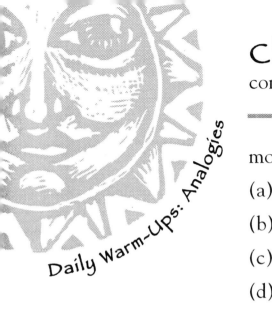

Choose the correct word pair to complete the analogy.

movie : cinema :: _____ : _____

(a) match : arena

(b) concert : orchestra

(c) rally : cause

(d) course : obstacle

Write the relationship sentence you used to complete this analogy.

Choose the correct word to complete the analogy.

intricate : simple :: satiated : _____

(a) satisfied

(b) bewildered

(c) unhappy

(d) hungry

54

Write the relationship sentence you used to complete this analogy.

Complete the analogy by choosing the correct answer from the word bank.

drink	shard	fracture	metal	clothing

_____ : glass :: scrap : fabric

Write the relationship sentence you used to complete this analogy.

55

Choose the correct word pair to complete the analogy.

water : soak :: _____ : _____

(a) air : inflate

(b) soil : grow

(c) concrete : dwell

(d) sun : bathe

56

Write the relationship sentence you used to complete this analogy.

Fill in the blank to complete the analogy.
There are many correct answers.

---

dollar : currency :: _____ : flower

Write the relationship sentence you used to complete this analogy.

.

57

© 2002 J. Weston Walch, Publisher

Choose the correct word to complete the analogy.

soothe : pacify :: _____ : annoy

(a) endanger

(b) ameliorate

(c) assail

(d) irk

58

Write the relationship sentence you used to complete this analogy.

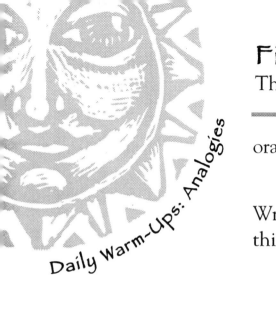

Fill in the blank to complete the analogy.
There is more than one correct answer.

orator : _____ :: builder : construct

Write the relationship sentence you used to complete this analogy.

59

Choose the correct word pair to complete the analogy.

annoyed : irate :: _____ : _____

(a) sunny : mild

(b) paltry : meager

(c) unkind : helpful

(d) confused : bewildered

What type of analogy is this?

Daily Warm-Ups: Analogies

© 2002 J. Weston Walch, Publisher

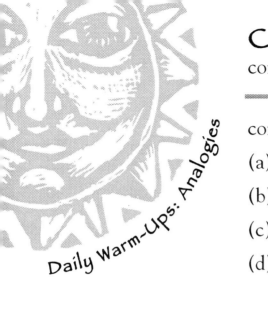

Choose the correct word to complete the analogy.

composer : music :: choreographer : _____

(a) dance

(b) stage

(c) exercise

(d) art

Write the relationship sentence you used to complete this analogy.

61

Fill in the blanks to complete the analogy.

There are many correct answers.

_____

compress : smaller :: _____ : _____

Write the relationship sentence you used to complete this analogy.

62

Choose the correct word to

complete the analogy.

lucid : _____ :: strict : lax

(a) rich

(b) murky

(c) entwined

(d) unable

Write the relationship sentence
you used to complete this analogy.

63

Choose the correct word pair to complete the analogy.

happiness : emotion :: _____ : _____

(a) horror : glee

(b) belief : faith

(c) sight : sense

(d) taste : pleasure

64

What type of analogy is this?

Complete the analogy by choosing
the correct answer from the word bank.

| courage knowledge disbelief |
| unhappiness disproportion |

novice : inexperience :: skeptic : _____

Write the relationship sentence you used to
complete this analogy.

Choose the correct word to complete the analogy.

embark : return :: initiate : _____

(a) deride

(b) imply

(c) incite

(d) conclude

66

Write the relationship sentence you used to complete this analogy.

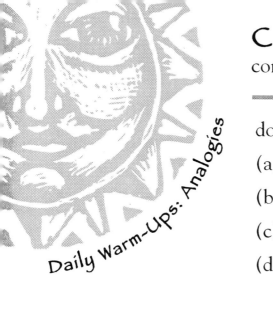

Choose the correct word to complete the analogy.

---

douse : fire :: _____ : thirst

(a) intensify

(b) deplete

(c) quench

(d) squelch

Write the relationship sentence you used to complete this analogy.

67

Fill in the blanks to complete the analogy.

There are many correct answers.

journalist : report :: _____ : _____

Write the relationship sentence you used to complete this analogy.

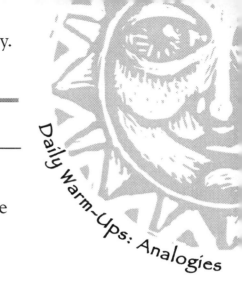

68

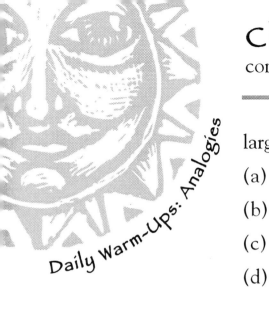

Choose the correct word pair to complete the analogy.

large : immense :: _____ : _____

(a) civil : human

(b) unkind : cruel

(c) tiny : enormous

(d) uninformed : knowledgeable

Write the relationship sentence you used to complete this analogy.

.

69

Complete the analogy by choosing
the correct answer from the word bank.

| polished | angry | tousled | troubled | tamed |

disheveled : _____ :: abrupt : curt

Write the relationship sentence you used to complete
this analogy.

70

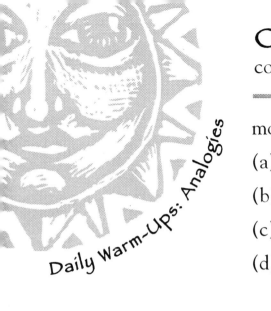

Choose the correct word pair to complete the analogy.

monarch : kingdom :: _____ : _____

(a) president : democracy

(b) criminal : penitentiary

(c) serf : plantation

(d) player : opponent

Write the relationship sentence you used to complete this analogy.

Fill in the blanks to complete the analogy.

There are many correct answers.

_____

_____ : _____ :: tiff : riot

Write the relationship sentence you used to complete this analogy.

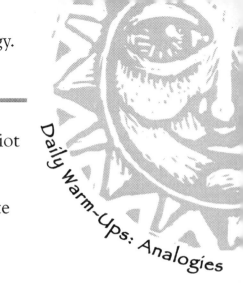

72

Choose the correct word pair to complete the analogy.

sailor : ship :: _____ : _____

(a) soldier : army

(b) astronaut : rocket

(c) commuter : traffic

(d) farmer : field

Write the relationship sentence you used to complete this analogy.

© 2002 J. Weston Walch, Publisher

Complete the analogy by choosing

the correct answer from the word bank.

---

affect   embezzle   confront   insist   assume

praise : deride :: _____ : avoid

What type of analogy is this?

74

Fill in the blanks to complete the analogy.

There are many correct answers.

---

astronomer : telescope :: _____ : _____

Write the relationship sentence you used to complete this analogy.

© 2002 J. Weston Walch, Publisher

Write a relationship sentence for the analogy below.

cub : bear :: calf : cow

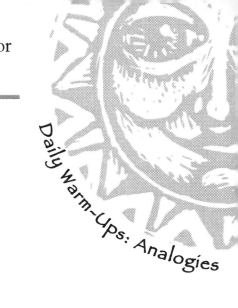

76

Choose the correct word to

complete the analogy.

alter : change :: _____ : scale

(a) dole

(b) heft

(c) mark

(d) climb

Write the relationship sentence you
used to complete this analogy.

77

Choose the correct word pair to complete the analogy.

fish : school :: _____ : _____

(a) cow : pasture

(b) sheep : flock

(c) eagle : nest

(d) frog : toad

78

What type of analogy is this?

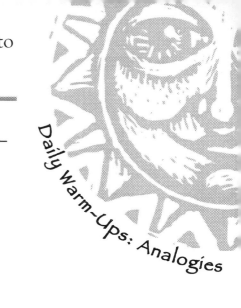

Complete the analogy by choosing
the correct answer from the word bank.

| snow | pole | winter | lodge | event |

skater : ice :: skier : _____

Write the relationship sentence you
used to complete this analogy.

79

Choose the correct word pair to complete the analogy.

collect : hoard :: _____ : _____

(a) travel : sightsee

(b) remind : nag

(c) suspect : believe

(d) honor : obey

80

Write the relationship sentence you used to complete this analogy.

Fill in the blank to complete the analogy.

There are many correct answers.

turtle : amphibian :: _____ : mammal

Write the relationship sentence you used to complete
this analogy.

81

Choose the correct word pair to complete the analogy.

---

famine : food :: _____ : _____

(a) glut : supply

(b) feast : gourmet

(c) pollution : air

(d) drought : water

82

Write the relationship sentence you used to complete this analogy.

Choose the correct word to

complete the analogy.

---

gusto : _____ :: happiness : glee

(a) anger

(b) enthusiasm

(c) confusion

(d) insanity

Write the relationship sentence you
used to complete this analogy.

83

Write a relationship sentence for the analogy below.

hat : head :: shoe : foot

84

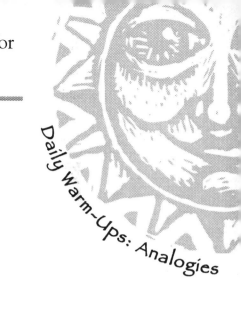

Choose the correct word pair to complete the analogy.

trigger : reaction :: _____ : _____

(a) triumph : competition

(b) explain : question

(c) aspire : hope

(d) ignite : fire

What type of analogy is this?

85

Choose the correct word to complete the analogy.

benefactor : give :: mimic : _____

(a) ape

(b) imply

(c) display

(d) pertain

86

Write the relationship sentence you used to complete this analogy.

Choose the correct word pair to complete the analogy.

---

expert : knowledge :: _____ : _____

(a) police : evidence

(b) lion : cubs

(c) saint : virtue

(d) thief : goods

Write the relationship sentence you used to complete this analogy.

87

© 2002 J. Weston Walch, Publisher

Fill in the blanks to complete the analogy.

There are many correct answers.

---

armor : protect :: _____ : _____

Write the relationship sentence you used to complete this analogy.

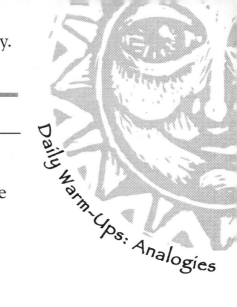

88

Complete the analogy by choosing

the correct answer from the word bank.

---

brave	unproductive	indispensable
	embarrassed	tired

timid : bold :: _____ : industrious

Write the relationship sentence you
used to complete this analogy.

89

Fill in the blanks to complete the analogy.

There are many correct answers.

---

plant : reap :: _____ : _____

Write the relationship sentence you used to complete this analogy.

90

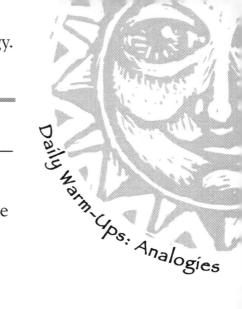

Choose the correct word to complete the analogy.

circumference : circle :: _____ : square

(a) perimeter

(b) area

(c) radius

(d) boundary

What type of analogy is this?

91

Choose the correct word pair to complete the analogy.

sketch : painting :: _____ : _____

(a) paper : brush

(b) outline : essay

(c) contrast : light

(d) concept : attempt

Write the relationship sentence you used to complete this analogy.

92

Fill in the blanks to complete the analogy.

There are many correct answers.

---

tree : orchard :: _____ : _____

Write the relationship sentence you used to complete this analogy.

Choose the correct word pair to

complete the analogy.

---

tiger : feline :: _____ : _____

(a) bear : canine

(b) ant : marsupial

(c) owl : lupine

(d) cow : bovine

94

Write the relationship sentence you used to complete this analogy.

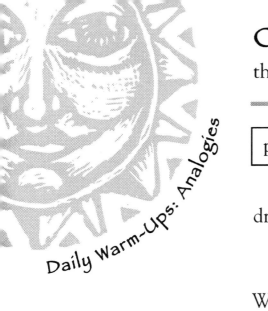

Complete the analogy by choosing

the correct answer from the word bank.

| prepared | able | foolish | uncomfortable | finished |

drowsy : alert :: _____ : inept

Write the relationship sentence you
used to complete this analogy.

95

Choose the correct word pair to complete the analogy.

hunter : prey :: _____ : _____

(a) swimmer : lane

(b) miner : ore

(c) competitor : defeat

(d) student : book

What type of analogy is this?

96

Fill in the blanks to complete the analogy.

There are many correct answers.

wedge : pie :: _____ : _____

Write the relationship sentence you used to complete this analogy.

97

Fill in the blank to complete the analogy.
There are many correct answers.

hopeful : discouraged :: _____ : honest

Write the relationship sentence you used to complete this analogy.

98

Choose the correct word pair to complete the analogy.

sailor : ocean :: _____ : _____

(a) farmer : field

(b) doctor : town

(c) banker : money

(d) tailor : clothes

Write the relationship sentence you used to complete this analogy.

© 2002 J. Weston Walch, Publisher

Fill in the blanks to complete the analogy.

There are many correct answers.

diamond : gem :: _____ : _____

Write the relationship sentence you used to complete this analogy.

100

Choose the correct word to

complete the analogy.

---

sip : guzzle :: _____ : gulp

(a) gobble

(b) prepare

(c) nibble

(d) nudge

Write the relationship sentence you used to complete this analogy.

101

Fill in the blank to complete the analogy.

There may be more than one correct answer.

---

compass : _____ :: sundial : time

Write the relationship sentence you used to complete this analogy.

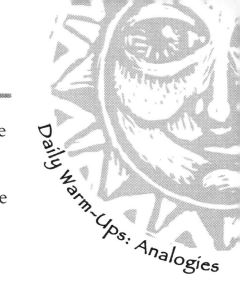

102

Complete the analogy by choosing
the correct answer from the word bank.

---

happy   angry   sorry   amused   confused

frequent : often :: contrite : _____

Write the relationship sentence you
used to complete this analogy.

Choose the correct word to complete the analogy.

_____

_____: spry :: juvenile : young

(a) weak

(b) hurt

(c) nimble

(d) aged

What type of analogy is this?

104

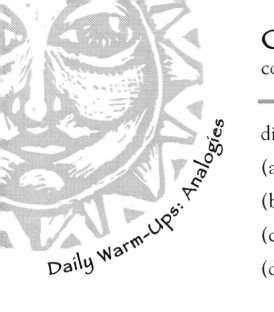

Choose the correct word pair to complete the analogy.

diver : pool :: _____ : _____

(a) skater : ice

(b) skier : pole

(c) hiker : shoe

(d) swimmer : towel

Write the relationship sentence you used to complete this analogy.

105

© 2002 J. Weston Walch, Publisher

Fill in the blanks to complete the analogy.

There are many correct answers.

---

barber : razor :: _____ : _____

Write the relationship sentence you used to complete this analogy.

106

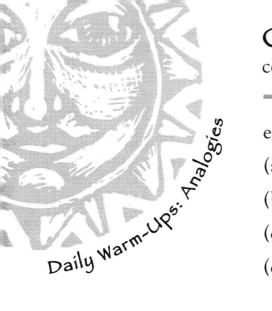

Choose the correct word to

complete the analogy.

enrich : fertile :: deplete : _____

(a) futile

(b) useful

(c) barren

(d) renewed

Write the relationship sentence you
used to complete this analogy.

107

Choose the correct word to complete the analogy.

vaccine : prevention :: medicine : _____

(a) doctor

(b) illness

(c) impairment

(d) treatment

What type of analogy is this?

108

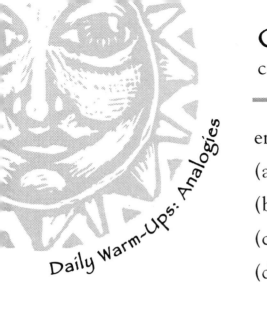

Choose the correct word to complete the analogy.

embellish : ornate :: pare : _____

(a) spartan

(b) unbelievable

(c) fancy

(d) nonexistent

Write the relationship sentence you used to complete this analogy.

109

© 2002 J. Weston Walch, Publisher

Choose the correct word pair to complete the analogy.

digit : number :: _____ : _____

(a) letter : word

(b) paper : pen

(c) equation : sum

(d) subject : exam

110

Write the relationship sentence you used to complete this analogy.

Fill in the blank to complete the analogy.

There are several correct answers.

ajar : open :: _____ : large

Write the relationship sentence you used to complete this analogy.

Daily Warm-Ups: Analogies

Choose the correct word pair to complete the analogy.

fork : utensil :: _____ : _____

(a) plant : animal

(b) fence : barrier

(c) pencil : pen

(d) tree : forest

Write the relationship sentence you used to complete this analogy.

Choose the correct word pair to complete the analogy.

welder : heat :: _____ : _____

(a) bricklayer : wall

(b) carver : statue

(c) teacher : chalk

(d) tailor : thread

What type of analogy is this?

113

Fill in the blank to complete the analogy.
There are several correct answers.

---

small : miniscule :: afraid : _____

Write the relationship sentence you used to complete this analogy.

114

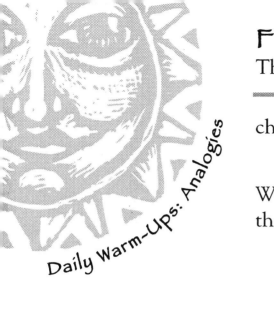

Fill in the blanks to complete the analogy.

There are many correct answers.

chef : meals :: _____ : _____

Write the relationship sentence you used to complete this analogy.

115

Complete the analogy by choosing
the correct answer from the word bank.

---

bereaved	bewildered	carefree	cognizant	alert

solemn : serious :: _____ : confused

Write the relationship sentence you used to complete
this analogy.

116

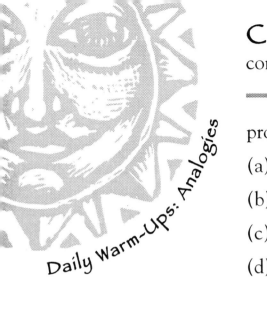

Choose the correct word pair to complete the analogy.

prompter : remind :: _____ : _____

(a) juggler : throw

(b) librarian : read

(c) monitor : watch

(d) detective : hide

Write the relationship sentence you used to complete this analogy.

117

Fill in the blanks to complete the analogy.

There are many correct answers.

---

lawyer : court :: _____ : _____

Write the relationship sentence you used to complete this analogy.

118

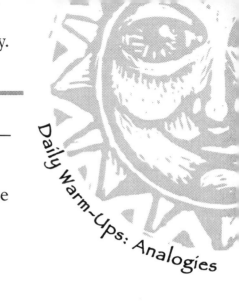

Choose the correct word pair to complete the analogy.

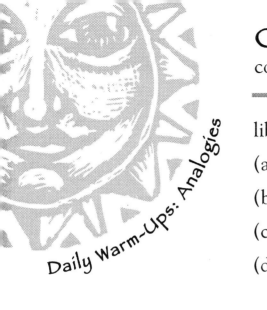

liberated : freedom :: _____ : _____

(a) chastised : hope

(b) encouraged : fear

(c) allowed : prevention

(d) emboldened : bravery

Write the relationship sentence you used to complete this analogy.

.

119

Complete the analogy by choosing
the correct answer from the word bank.

| stingy | ugly | angry | sulky | hungry |

miser : _____ :: pacifist : peaceful

What type of analogy is this?

120

Choose the correct word pair to

complete the analogy.

stars : constellation :: _____ : _____

(a) flowers : bouquet

(b) cars : highway

(c) dogs : kennel

(d) fish : pond

Write the relationship sentence you
used to complete this analogy.

121

Choose the correct word to complete the analogy.

malodorous : fragrant :: _____ : handsome

(a) intelligent

(b) comely

(c) unsightly

(d) insipid

Write the relationship sentence you used to complete this analogy.

Fill in the blanks to complete the analogy.

There are many correct answers.

belt : cinch :: _____ : _____

Write the relationship sentence you used to complete this analogy.

Choose the correct word to

complete the analogy.

---

praise : encouraged :: scold : _____

(a) chastened

(b) embittered

(c) endeared

(d) entitled

124

Write the relationship sentence you used to complete this analogy.

Fill in the blank to complete the analogy.

There are many correct answers.

---

human : biped :: _____ : quadruped

What type of analogy is this?

© 2002 J. Weston Walch, Publisher

Complete the analogy by choosing
the correct answer from the word bank.

decide	report	intrigue	instigate	instill

detective : investigate :: journalist : _____

Write the relationship sentence you used to complete
this analogy.

126

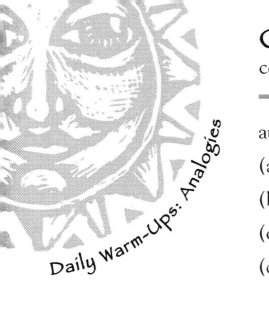

Choose the correct word to complete the analogy.

audio : hearing :: tactile : _____

(a) vision

(b) taste

(c) touch

(d) smell

Write the relationship sentence you used to complete this analogy.

127

Choose the correct word pair to complete the analogy.

---

lime : fruit :: _____ : _____

(a) rice : bean

(b) truck : traffic

(c) easel : art

(d) schooner : ship

What type of analogy is this?

Fill in the blanks to complete the analogy.

There are many correct answers.

wolf : pack :: _____ : _____

Write the relationship sentence you used to complete this analogy.

129

Choose the correct word to complete the analogy.

referee : game :: judge : _____

(a) court

(b) gavel

(c) jury

(d) justice

130

Write the relationship sentence you used to complete this analogy.

Complete the analogy by choosing the correct answer from the word bank.

| intense | loose | riled | delighted | carefree |

rigid : lax :: _____ : calm

Write the relationship sentence you used to complete this analogy.

.

131

© 2002 J. Weston Walch, Publisher

Choose the correct word pair to complete the analogy.

aviator : airplane :: _____ : _____

(a) driver : engine

(b) tire : truck

(c) farmer : field

(d) engineer : train

Write the relationship sentence you used to complete this analogy.

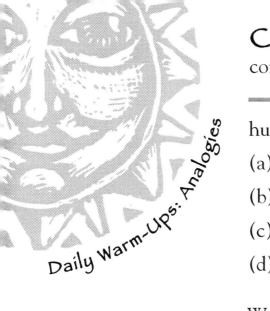

Choose the correct word to

complete the analogy.

hut : dwelling :: _____ : clothing

(a) fashion

(b) store

(c) cloak

(d) needle

Write the relationship sentence you used to complete this analogy.

133

Complete the analogy by choosing
the correct answer from the word bank.

---

gullible	fanciful	suspicious	trustworthy	special

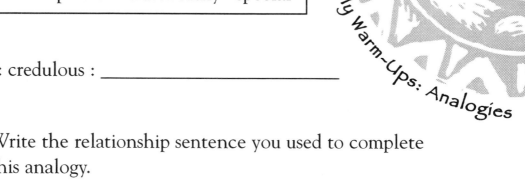

eccentric : odd :: credulous : _____

Write the relationship sentence you used to complete this analogy.

134

Fill in the blank to complete the analogy.

There are several correct answers.

---

sleepy : exhausted :: hungry : _____

Write the relationship sentence you used to complete this analogy.

135

Choose the correct word pair to complete the analogy.

skater : rink :: _____ : _____

(a) dancer : tutu

(b) actor : stage

(c) singer : voice

(d) mime : gesture

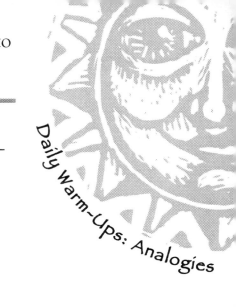

What type of analogy is this?

136

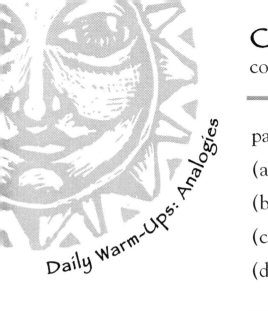

Choose the correct word to complete the analogy.

partition : sectioned :: irrigate : _____

(a) nourished

(b) useable

(c) healthy

(d) hydrated

Write the relationship sentence you used to complete this analogy.

Choose the correct word to complete the analogy.

suffragist : vote :: abolitionist : _____

(a) education

(b) compensation

(c) freedom

(d) truth

138

Write the relationship sentence you used to complete this analogy.

Choose the correct word pair to complete the analogy.

delegate : represent :: _____ : _____

(a) illustrator : depict

(b) president : impeach

(c) lawyer : convict

(d) guard : allow

Write the relationship sentence you used to complete this analogy.

139

Fill in the blanks to complete the analogy.

There are several correct answers.

---

disagreement : assent :: _____ : _____

Write the relationship sentence you used to complete this analogy.

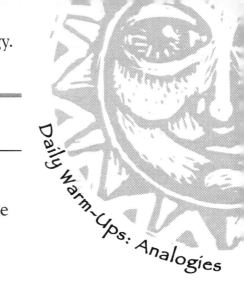

140

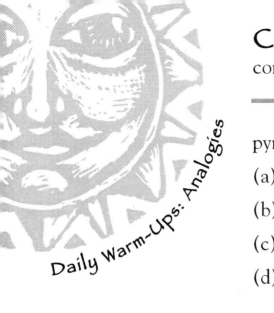

Choose the correct word to

complete the analogy.

pyramid : structure :: mesa : _____

(a) oasis

(b) sand

(c) desert

(d) landform

Write the relationship sentence you
used to complete this analogy.

141

Choose the correct word pair to complete the analogy.

patriot : treasonous :: _____ : _____

(a) scholar : learned

(b) believer : doubtful

(c) prophet : insightful

(d) loner : spiteful

What type of analogy is this?

142

Fill in the blanks to complete the analogy.

There are several correct answers.

gardener : hoe :: _____ : _____

Write the relationship sentence you used to complete this analogy.

143

Choose the correct word pair to complete the analogy.

compass : direction :: _____ : _____

(a) barometer : pressure

(b) thermometer : weather

(c) microscope : germ

(d) telescope : vision

Write the relationship sentence you used to complete this analogy.

144

Complete the analogy by choosing
the correct answer from the word bank.

excited humble jaded credulous courageous

acrid : sweet :: _____ : enthusiastic

Write the relationship sentence you
used to complete this analogy.

145

Choose the correct word to complete the analogy.

stanza : poem :: paragraph : _____

(a) essay

(b) subject

(c) illustration

(d) volume

146

Write the relationship sentence you used to complete this analogy.

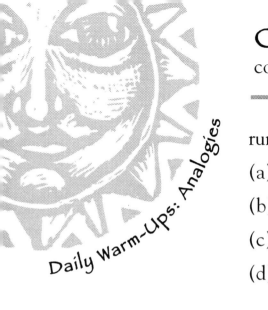

Choose the correct word pair to complete the analogy.

runner : speedy :: _____ : _____

(a) singer : smart

(b) scientist : discerning

(c) scholar : learned

(d) accountant : artistic

Write the relationship sentence you used to complete this analogy.

147

Choose the correct word pair to complete the analogy.

---

scientist : laboratory :: _____ : _____

(a) writer : newspaper

(b) photographer : darkroom

(c) racer : automobile

(d) painter : color

148

What type of analogy is this?

Choose the correct word to

complete the analogy.

---

pleased : overjoyed :: sad : _____

(a) uncertain

(b) delighted

(c) miffed

(d) miserable

Write the relationship sentence you
used to complete this analogy.

149

Complete the analogy by choosing

the correct answer from the word bank.

---

unaware watchful pert petty imaginative

_____ : alert :: unoriginal : trite

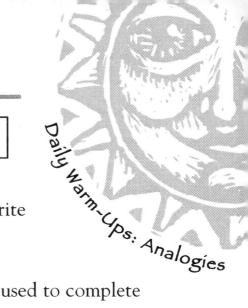

Write the relationship sentence you used to complete this analogy.

150

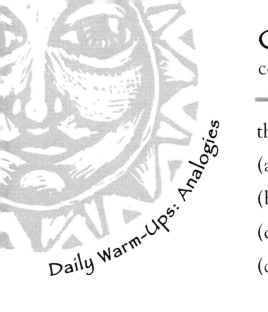

Choose the correct word to complete the analogy.

thin : gaunt :: thirsty : _____

(a) tired

(b) hungry

(c) quenched

(d) parched

Write the relationship sentence you used to complete this analogy.

151

Choose the correct word pair to complete the analogy.

study : test :: _____ : _____

(a) rehearse : play

(b) relax : marathon

(c) criticize : book

(d) imply : speech

152

Write the relationship sentence you used to complete this analogy.

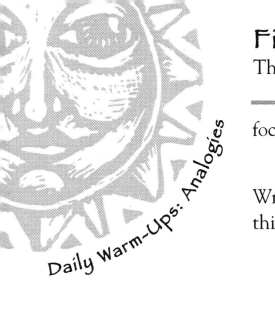

Fill in the blank to complete the analogy.

There may be several correct answers.

focused : distracted :: _____ : harmful

Write the relationship sentence you used to complete this analogy.

153

© 2002 J. Weston Walch, Publisher

Choose the correct word pair to complete the analogy.

listen : eavesdrop :: _____ : _____

(a) speak : shout

(b) reach : hit

(c) look : spy

(d) touch : grip

What type of analogy is this?

154

Choose the correct word to

complete the analogy.

composer : symphony :: _____ : sonnet

(a) painter

(b) poet

(c) musician

(d) photographer

Write the relationship sentence you
used to complete this analogy.

.

Fill in the blanks to complete the analogy.

There are many correct answers.

---

morose : cheerful :: _____ : _____

Write the relationship sentence you used to complete this analogy.

156

Choose the correct word pair to complete the analogy.

gaggle : geese :: _____ : _____

(a) stall : horse

(b) ocean : whale

(c) flock : sheep

(d) bank : river

Write the relationship sentence you used to complete this analogy.

© 2002 J. Weston Walch, Publisher

Choose the correct word to

complete the analogy.

---

mathematician : calculator :: navigator : _____

(a) map

(b) country

(c) terrain

(d) pilot

158

Write the relationship sentence you used to complete this analogy.

.

Complete the analogy by choosing
the correct answer from the word bank.

| absolute | infinite | improbable | sure | definite |

assured : uncertain :: likely : _____

Write the relationship sentence you used to complete this analogy.

159

Fill in the blank to complete the analogy.
There may be more than one correct answer.

---

nomadic : wandering :: mistaken : _____

What type of analogy is this?

160

Choose the correct word pair to complete the analogy.

painting : gallery :: _____ : _____

(a) violin : cello

(b) tome : library

(c) artifact : history

(d) song : vocalist

Write the relationship sentence you used to complete this analogy.

161

Choose the correct word pair to complete the analogy.

bud : blossom :: _____ : _____

(a) leaf : flutter

(b) caterpillar : march

(c) lawn : mow

(d) egg : hatch

162

Write the relationship sentence you used to complete this analogy.

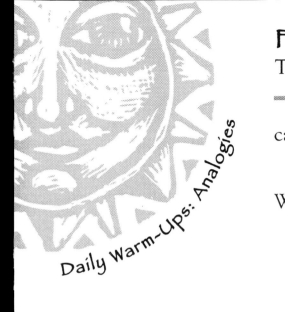

Fill in the blank to complete the analogy.

There may be more than one correct answer.

cactus : desert :: _____ : prairie

What type of analogy is this?

Choose the correct word pair to
complete the analogy.

---

ship : fleet :: _____ : _____

(a) soldier : platoon

(b) egg : chicken

(c) calendar : year

(d) engine : track

Write the relationship sentence you used to complete
this analogy.

164

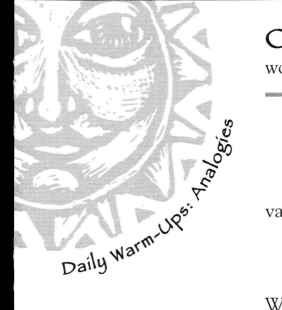

Choose the best answer from the word bank to complete the analogy.

| encode   repeat   reveal   subvert   betray |

vault : store :: cipher : _____

Write the relationship sentence you used to complete this analogy.

Choose the correct word to complete the analogy.

artery : blood :: _____ : water

(a) sink

(b) fall

(c) pipe

(d) glass

Write the relationship sentence you used to complete this analogy.

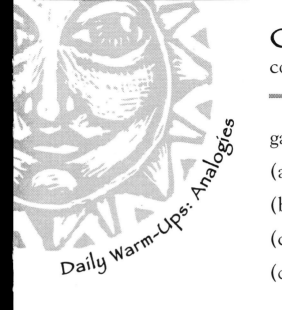

Choose the correct word pair to complete the analogy.

gardener : trowel :: _____ : _____

(a) hiker : hill

(b) competitor : strategy

(c) traveler : direction

(d) farmer : plow

Write the relationship sentence you used to complete this analogy.

© 2002 J. Weston Walch, Publisher

Complete the analogy by choosing

the best answer from the word bank.

biologist   herbivore   botanist   vegetable   rainforest

carnivore : meat :: _____ : plant

Write the relationship sentence you used to complete
this analogy.

168

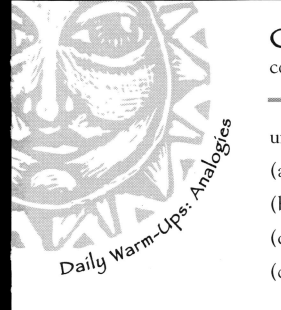

Choose the correct word pair to complete the analogy.

unmask : reveal :: _____ : _____

(a) decrease : increase

(b) impair : dislike

(c) interpret : cloak

(d) costume : disguise

What type of analogy is this?

© 2002 J. Weston Walch, Publisher

Fill in the blanks to complete the analogy.

There are many correct answers.

---

impede : hinder :: _____ : _____

Write the relationship sentence you used to complete this analogy.

170

Choose the correct word pair to complete the analogy.

state : insist :: _____ : _____

(a) decry : support

(b) believe : doubt

(c) hope : yearn

(d) reveal : hide

Write the relationship sentence you used to complete this analogy.

Complete the analogy by choosing

the best answer from the word bank.

dictatorial	friendly	political	severe	legal

criminal : illegal :: tyrant : _____

Write the relationship sentence you used to complete this analogy.

172

Daily Warm-Ups: Analogies

Choose the correct word pair to complete the analogy.

ebb : tide :: _____ : moon

(a) wane

(b) revolve

(c) rotate

(d) shine

Write the relationship sentence you used to complete this analogy.

Fill in the blanks to complete the analogy.
There are many correct answers.

---

prove : belie :: _____ : _____

Write the relationship sentence you used to complete this analogy.

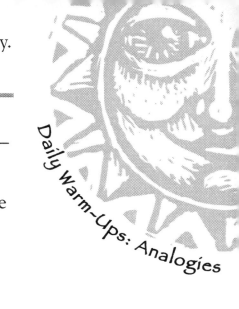

174

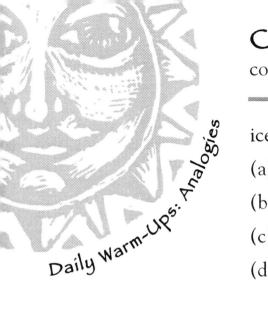

Choose the correct word pair to complete the analogy.

ice cube : glacier :: _____ : _____

(a) mineral : ore

(b) pebble : boulder

(c) drop : bucket

(d) fabric : bolt

Write the relationship sentence you used to complete this analogy.

175

Fill in the blanks to complete the analogy.

There are many correct answers.

counselor : advise :: _____ : _____

Write the relationship sentence you used to complete this analogy.

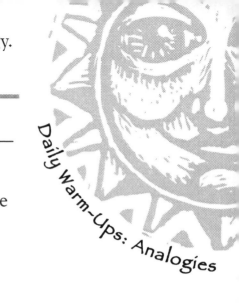

176

Complete the analogy by choosing

the correct answer from the word bank.

respect	merriment	insolence
	degradation	kindness

mirth : happiness :: impertinence : _____

Write the relationship sentence you
used to complete this analogy.

Choose the correct word pair to complete the analogy.

explanation : clarify :: _____ : _____

(a) foreword : recap

(b) picture : replace

(c) example : illustrate

(d) omission : emphasize

What type of analogy is this?

Choose the correct word pair to complete the analogy.

oil : viscous :: _____ : _____

(a) rain : acid

(b) water : fluid

(c) lemon : citrus

(d) wood : ignitable

Write the relationship sentence you used to complete this analogy.

179

Choose the correct word to

complete the analogy.

fortify : strengthen :: mollify : _____

(a) entertain

(b) bewitch

(c) attempt

(d) soothe

Write the relationship sentence you used to complete
this analogy.

6. (c); description : greater degree
7. (a); object : function
8. Answers will vary. Accept any answer that completes the object : category relationship (for example, maple).
9. (d); word : antonym
10. Accept any answer that completes the word : synonym relationship (for example, hurry : hasten).
11. (b)
12. (c)
13. sculptor; agent : object
14. (d)
15. Accept any answer in which there is an object/person : description relationship (for example, pauper : poor).
16. (c)
17. Accept any answer that completes the action : greater degree relationship (for example, stare).
18. (b)
19. (d)
20. (d); word : synonym
21. Accept any answer that completes the cause : effect relationship (for example, actions : consequences).
22. (a)
23. (b)
24. Accept any answer that completes the object : location relationship (for example, horse : stall).
25. (d); object : category
26. Accept any answer that completes the word : synonym relationship (for example, delight : happiness).
27. (c); agent : object
28. vehicle
29. (c)
30. Accept any answer that completes the description : greater degree relationship (for example, breeze : gust).

31. (a)
32. halt
33. Accept any answer that completes the object : description relationship (for example, lush).
34. (c); word : antonym
35. (b)
36. (a); agent : action
37. podium
38. Accept any answer that completes the part : whole relationship (for example, chorus).
39. (c)
40. Accept any answer that completes the word : synonym relationship (for example, obliterate : destroy).
41. (d)
42. (a); person : location
43. (c)
44. Accept any answer that completes the agent : action relationship (for example, spokesperson : represent).
45. (b)
46. oversee
47. Accept any adjective that completes the object : description relationship (for example, humorous).
48. Accept any answer that completes the word : antonym relationship (for example, flimsy : sturdy).
49. (c)
50. (b)
51. understanding
52. Accept any answer that completes the part : whole relationship (for example, soldier : army).
53. (a)
54. (d)
55. shard
56. (a)

57. Accept any answer that completes the object : category relationship (for example, tulip).
58. (d)
59. Accept any verb that completes the agent : action relationship (for example, speak).
60. (d); description : greater degree
61. (a)
62. Accept any answer that completes the cause : effect relationship (for example, expand : larger).
63. (b)
64. (c); object : category
65. disbelief
66. (d)
67. (c)
68. Accept any answer that completes the agent : action relationship (for example, professor : teach).
69. (b)
70. tousled
71. (a)
72. Accept any answer that completes the object : greater degree relationship (for example, tap : shove).
73. (b)
74. confront; word : antonym
75. Accept any answer that completes the agent : object relationship (for example, musician : instrument).
76. Accept answers as close as possible to A cub *is a baby* bear, *as a* calf *is a baby* cow.
77. (d)
78. (b); part : whole
79. snow
80. (b)
81. Accept any type of mammal (for example, monkey).
82. (d)

83. (b)
84. Accept any answer that is similar to A hat is *worn on the* head, *as a* shoe *is worn on the* foot.
85. (d); cause : effect
86. (a)
87. (c)
88. Accept any answer that completes the object : function relationship (for example, food : nourish).
89. unproductive
90. Accept any answer that completes the cause : effect relationship (for example, exercise : strengthen).
91. (a); part : whole
92. (b)
93. Accept any answer that completes the object : location relationship (for example, animal : menagerie). .
94. (d)

95. able
96. (b); agent : object
97. Accept any answer that completes the part : whole relationship (for example, slice : loaf).
98. Accept any answer that completes the word : antonym relationship (for example, untruthful).
99. (a)
100. Accept any answer that completes the object : category relationship (for example, apple : fruit).
101. (c)
102. Accept *direction* or anything similar.
103. sorry
104. (c)
105. (a)
106. Accept any answer that completes the agent : object relationship (for example, tailor : needle).

107. (c)
108. (d); object : category
109. (a)
110. (a)
111. Accept any answer that completes the word : synonym relationship (for example, immense).
112. (b)
113. (d); agent : object
114. Accept any answer that completes the description : greater degree relationship (for example, terrified).
115. Accept any answer that completes the agent : object relationship (for example, writer : stories).
116. bewildered
117. (c)
118. Accept any answer that completes the person : location relationship (for example, teacher : classroom).

119. (d)
120. stingy; person : description
121. (a)
122. (c)
123. Accept any answer that completes the object : function relationship (for example, helmet : protect).
124. (a)
125. Accept any answer that completes the object/person : category relationship (for example, cow).
126. report
127. (c)
128. (d); object : category
129. Accept any answer that completes the part : whole relationship (for example, bird : flock).
130. (a)
131. riled
132. (d)

Answer Key

133. (c)
134. gullible
135. Accept any answer that completes the description : greater degree relationship (for example, famished).
136. (b); person : location
137. (d)
138. (c)
139. (a)
140. Accept any answer that completes the word : antonym relationship (for example, harmony : discord).
141. (d)
142. (b); word : antonym
143. Accept any answer that completes the agent : object relationship (for example, firefighter : hose).
144. (a)
145. jaded
146. (a)

147. (c)
148. (b); person : location
149. (d)
150. watchful
151. (d)
152. (a)
153. Accept any answer that completes the word : antonym relationship (for example, helpful).
154. (c); description : greater degree
155. (b)
156. Accept any answer that completes the word : antonym relationship (for example, agreeable : argumentative).
157. (c)
158. (a)
159. improbable
160. Accept any answer that completes the word : synonym relationship (for example, errant).

161. (b)
162. (d)
163. Accept any answer that completes the object : location relationship (for example, grass).
164. (a)
165. encode
166. (c)
167. (d)
168. herbivore
169. (d); word : synonym
170. Accept any answer that completes the word : synonym relationship (for example, aide : help).
171. (c)
172. dictatorial
173. (a)
174. Accept any answer that completes the word : antonym relationship (for example, affirm : deny).
175. (b)
176. Accept any answer that completes the agent : action relationship (for example, vendor : sell).
177. insolence
178. (c); object : function
179. (b)
180. (d)